The Library of the Nine Planets™

VENUS

R. K. Renfield

rosen
central™

The Rosen Publishing Group, Inc., New York

For Betty and Otto

Published in 2005 by The Rosen Publishing Group, Inc.
29 East 21st Street, New York, NY 10010

First Edition

Library of Congress Cataloging-in-Publication Data

Renfield, R. K.
Venus / by R. K. Renfield. — 1st ed.
   p. cm. — (The library of the nine planets)
Summary: Describes the characteristics of the planet Venus, discoveries made by space probes, and how the planet has played a role in the mythologies of many different cultures and civilizations.
Includes bibliographical references and index.
ISBN 1-4042-0175-0 (lib. bdg.)
1. Venus (Planet)–Juvenile literature. [1. Venus (Planet)]
I. Title. II. Series.

QB621.R46 2004
523.42–dc22

            2003022416

Manufactured in the United States of America

Cover image: The western Eistla Regio region of Venus

Contents

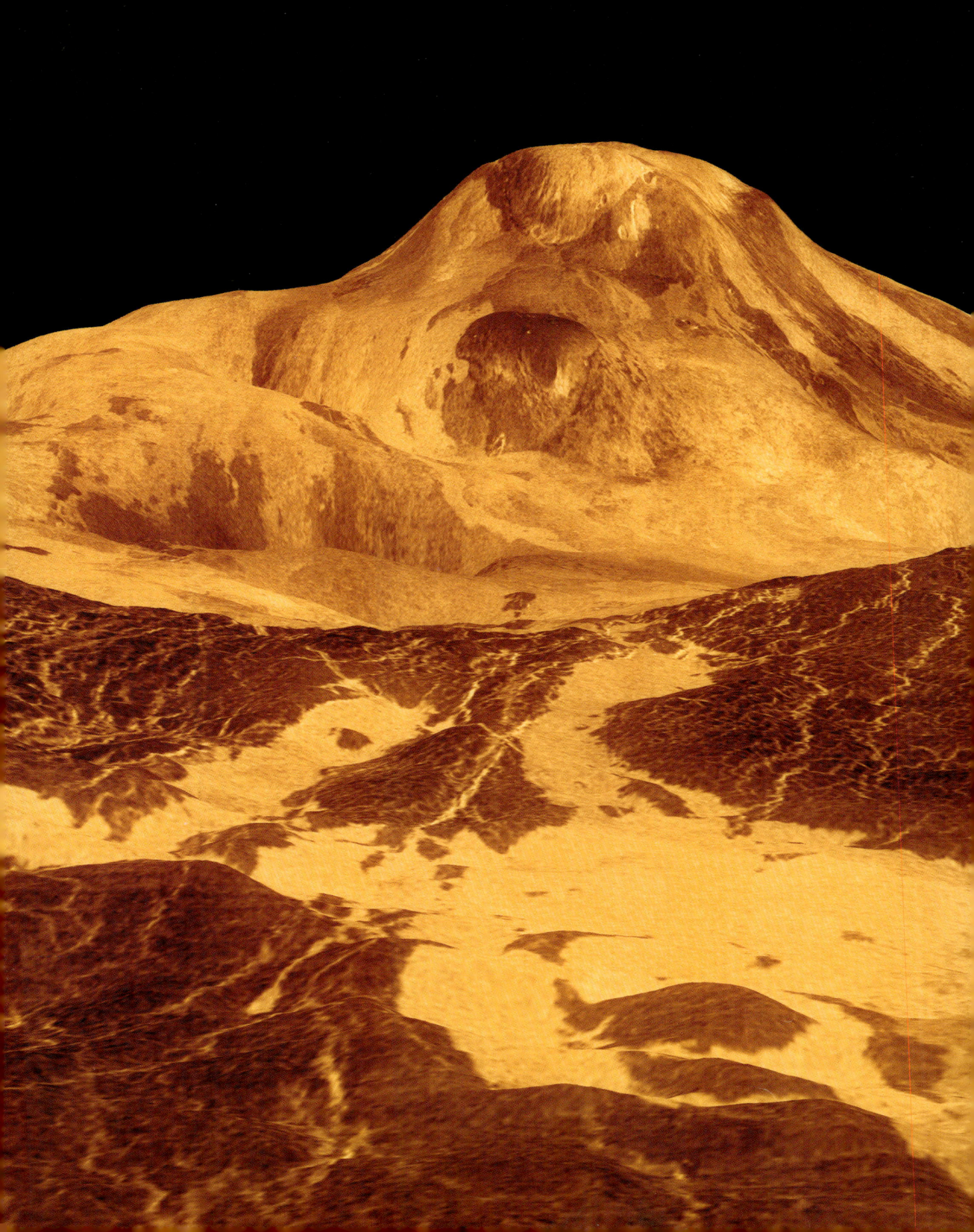

Introduction

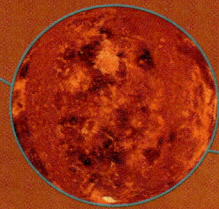

Venus has been known as the brightest object in the night sky since the beginning of recorded history. On clear nights, Venus is the first object to appear and is sometimes so luminous that its light casts very faint shadows on the ground on Earth. It has figured prominently in the mythologies of many cultures, including those of the Sumerians, Aztecs, Maya, and ancient Romans—the Romans named the planet after their goddess of love and beauty.

Before humankind had the technology to peer through the planet's atmosphere and see the surface below its cloud layers, Venus was considered Earth's sister. People imagined that Venus might have a hot surface of dense vegetation and continual warm rain, perhaps even resembling Earth's rain forests. It even seemed likely that Venus could support life.

We now know though that Venus's surface conditions are nothing like our own. The surface is hot enough to melt lead, and water (needed to support life as we know it) is found in only trace amounts.

Its clouds are made of sulfuric acid swirling in an atmosphere comprised mainly of

In Roman mythology, Venus is the goddess of love and beauty. She was originally a goddess of vegetation and of gardens and vineyards. She is shown here with Cupid, the Roman god of love, in this painting by Pompeo Girolamo Batoni.

carbon dioxide. The planet's heat and lack of a sufficient amount of water mean that there will never be any plants to convert that carbon dioxide into oxygen, which is needed for human habitation. In fact, Venus's surface conditions are hotter and even more hostile to life than those of Mercury, the closest planet to the Sun.

Venus's mass, size, and material composition, however, are very similar to Earth's. Although it has no significant amount of water now, Venus may have once had oceans. And though there is little hope of organic life developing there, planetary scientists are engaged in studying Venus in hopes of learning more about changes in Earth's climate. From ancient times to today, Venus has had a lot to teach us about the planet we call home.

One

An Eventful History

About 4.5 billion years ago, our solar system was formed. As the solar system was forming, the Sun's gravity pulled most of the heaviest materials, like iron, zinc, and nickel, in toward itself. Since these materials have a lot of mass, the Sun's gravity had a stronger pull on them, and they pulled closer inward than the less massive materials. They slowed down, eventually forming the cores of the terrestrial planets. The lighter materials, such as ice crystals and hydrogen, were farther away. They eventually formed Jupiter, Saturn, Uranus, and Neptune, which are known as the Gas Giants.

The nine planets of the solar system can be divided into two groups: the inner, or terrestrial planets of Mercury, Venus, Earth, and Mars; and the outer planets of Jupiter, Saturn, Uranus, Neptune, and Pluto.

Venus is the second planet from the Sun, larger than Mercury but smaller than Earth. Even though Venus resembles Earth very closely in its composition, it developed very differently as a planet. Many scientists believe that it may have had oceans at some point in its history, which evaporated because of its proximity to the Sun.

Stories and Myths

Humans have been fascinated with Venus since the beginning of recorded history, and the planet has played a role in the

Many ancient civilizations worshiped the planet Venus. The Pyramid of Kukulcan, shown here, was built by the Mayan people around AD 900 in the village of Chichén Itzá in southeast Mexico. Originally used as a calendar, it has 365 steps, one for each day in the calendar year.

mythologies of many different cultures and civilizations. To the Sumerians, the earliest-known human civilization, which was located in present-day Iraq, Venus was Ishtar, a goddess responsible for fertility on Earth. To the early Greeks, Venus was Phosphoros, the dawn-bearer. The present name, Venus, comes from the ancient Romans. They named the planet after Venus, their goddess of love and beauty.

Although Venus figures in the mythology of cultures all over the world, the planet plays a special role in the stories of the Maya, a civilization spreading through present-day Belize, Guatemala, and Mexico. From about 1500 BC to the sixteenth century AD, when they were conquered by invading Spanish conquistadores, the Maya were the most advanced of all the ancient astronomers.

The Maya named Venus Kukulcan and believed that the planet was the Sun's brother. In the Popol Vuh, the Mayan creation epic, Kukulcan and the Sun descend into the underworld to battle evil beings known as the Lords of Death. The Lords of Death devise many tests and trials to kill the brothers, but they are outwitted every time. Eventually, Kukulcan and the Sun defeat the Lords of Death, bringing the first dawn to Earth.

The Maya sacrificed scores of victims to Kukulcan every year. They also built observatory pyramids from which their astronomer priests could monitor the movements of the planet, which they recorded in great detail, and were able to predict the position of years into the future. The Maya also developed a calendar based on the movements of Venus. This calendar is so accurate that even today it is off by only two hours.

Unfortunately, invading conquistadores, who considered Mayan science and religion heretical, or nonreligious, destroyed almost all of the Maya's codexes, or books. Much of what we know about their ancient culture today comes from just four surviving codexes.

The Heliocentric Universe

Venus has led to several great astronomical discoveries. One of the most important functions Venus has played in history is its role as the planet that proved the theory of the heliocentric, or sun-centered, solar system.

For centuries, most people in the Western world believed in the model of the universe originated by the second-century AD scholar Ptolemy. Living in Alexandria, Egypt, Ptolemy devised an incredibly complicated system to explain the way the stars moved in the sky. This system placed Earth at the center of the solar system, with all heavenly bodies, including the Sun, revolving around it.

In the early seventeenth century, an Italian astronomer named Galileo Galilei observed that Venus had faint phases, just like the Moon. It also dramatically changed size, becoming very small when it was brightest. Galileo realized that this must mean that Venus's distance from Earth was not constant and that it must be orbiting the Sun. Galileo came forward with this information, but the world was not ready to hear that Earth was not the center of the universe. The Catholic Church had decided that the work of Galileo contradicted its description of the universe. Convicted of heresy, Galileo was placed under house arrest until his death in 1642.

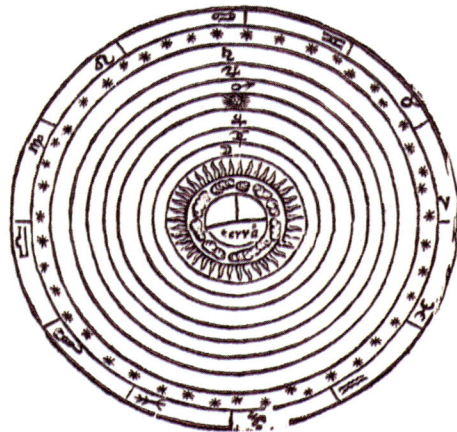

SYSTEMA PTOLEMAICVM.

Until the mid-sixteenth century, it was believed that Earth was the center of the universe. This diagram shows the view of the universe as proposed by the second-century philosopher Ptolemy. Earth, "terra," sits at the center. Moving outward are the Moon, Mercury, Venus, the Sun, Mars, Jupiter, Saturn, and the stars, including the star constellations.

A "Map" of Venus

Many astronomers gazed at Venus through their telescopes but produced little in the way of useful information. At best, they argued about their results among themselves. Then in 1667, an Italian astronomer named Giovanni Cassini recorded what he believed were details about the planet's surface. He also incorrectly estimated that it took Venus twenty-three hours and twenty-one minutes to complete a full rotation on its axis, or to complete one full day.

The first "map" of Venus's surface was created in 1726 by another Italian astronomer named Francesco Bianchini. Observing Venus through a telescope, he recorded and named features that he believed were oceans, continents, and landforms. Others also saw various surface features that they dutifully recorded. One of these scientists included an American astronomer named Percival Lowell, who was convinced that he saw canals on Venus. What these astronomers did not know was that Venus is completely enveloped in clouds that obscured any surface details. The surface features they recorded were actually just discolorations in the cloud cover.

The first significant discovery about Venus by use of a telescope was made in 1761 by Mikhail Vasilyevich Lomonosov. Lomonosov, a Russian astronomer, discovered that Venus had an atmosphere that hid its surface. In 1788, a German astronomer named Johann Hieronymus Schröter also came to this conclusion and also incorrectly estimated that Venus's day was twenty-three hours and twenty-one minutes long. The first person to correct this figure was an Italian astronomer named Giovanni Virginio Schiaparelli. Observing Venus between 1877 and 1878, he placed Venus's day as being 5,392 hours and 48 minutes long.

Better and better telescopes were devised as the decades passed, but there still was no way to observe Venus's surface. Was it a barren wasteland? Was it a lush, tropical paradise? Or was it something far stranger? It wasn't until the space age, when humankind developed the technology to send spacecraft and astronauts into outer space, that we would be able to get close enough to examine Venus in all of its glory.

The space race was a battle between the Soviet Union and the United States over which country could make the most advancements in space exploration. Soviet astronaut Yury Gagarin became the first person to orbit Earth on April 12, 1961. He made one complete revolution around Earth. His flight lasted a total of 108 minutes.

The Space Age

After World War II (1939–1945), the United States and the Soviet Union, who had been allies during the war, began to grow increasingly wary of each other due to their radically different political systems. The United States was a capitalist democracy. The Soviet Union, made up of present-day Russia and a number of surrounding republics, was a Communist dictatorship. The governments of both countries were worried that the system they opposed would spread and eventually take over the world. Although neither country directly attacked the other, both sides began stockpiling weapons, beginning a standoff known as the Cold War, which lasted until 1991.

For all of the fear and tension that the Cold War caused, it did have one miraculous by-product: the space race. In an effort to scientifically outdo each other, the United States and the Soviet Union began competing to see who could achieve the most "firsts" in the realm of space travel and exploration.

The Soviet Union put the first spacecraft, *Sputnik 1*, into orbit in 1957. *Sputnik 1*, which was about the size of a basketball, did little but orbit Earth and broadcast a relentless string of beeps. The Soviet Union also put the first living organism, a dog named Laika, into orbit aboard *Sputnik 2* in 1957; unfortunately, Laika did not make it back to Earth alive. A spacecraft called *Luna 3* made a trip around the Moon, photographing its far side in October 1959. The Soviet Union also sent the first human being into orbit, a young man by the name of Yury Gagarin, on April 12, 1961. Gagarin returned to Earth in one piece after his 108-minute flight and became a hero in his country.

Soviet Missions to Venus

The next step for the Soviet Union was to construct an interplanetary space vehicle. The logical place to send it was Venus since it is the closest planet to Earth. The Soviets would send a number of probes called Venera to Venus over the next two decades. Although there were a number of failures along the way, the Venera program provided many of the important early discoveries about Venus.

On February 12, 1961, the Soviets sent a space probe called *Venera 1* on its way to Venus. Unfortunately, after a successful launch and 4,650,000 miles (7,483,450 kilometers) of incident-free

The Venera missions, sent by the Soviet Union, were designed to explore Venus. *Venera 13* was one of many in the series of Venera missions. It was launched on October 30, 1981, and landed on Venus on March 1, 1982. *Venera 13* took this photograph of Venus's surface. Part of the spacecraft is visible in the foreground.

travel, *Venera 1* lost contact with Earth. *Venera 1* came within 62,000 miles (99,779 km) of Venus and eventually entered into an orbit around the Sun; it is believed to be still out there.

Other failures followed, but Soviet scientists didn't give up. *Venera 3* was launched on November 12, 1965, with the mission objective of landing on Venus's surface. *Venera 3* lost contact with Earth just as it made it through Venus's atmosphere. It crash-landed on the surface on March 1, 1966, and was destroyed.

In January 1969, *Venera 5* and *Venera 6* also entered the atmosphere, slowing their descents with parachutes and returning information. As Soviet scientists learned more about Venus and its toxic atmosphere, they were able to design spacecraft that could survive long enough in the intense heat and pressure to gather data.

Real success came in August 1970, when *Venera 7* was able to not only land on the surface but also send back information. For twenty-three minutes, it broadcast signals back to Earth, making it the first spacecraft to transmit data from another planet. Another breakthrough came from *Venera 9* and *Venera 10*. They landed on Venus in October 1975, and both sent back one photograph each.

There were sixteen Venera probes altogether, and the last one to land on Venus's surface was *Venera 14*, which touched down on March 5, 1982, with the intention of collecting soil samples for analysis. For fifty-six minutes, *Venera 14* endured a surface temperature of 869° Farenheit (465° Celsius) and an atmospheric pressure measured at ninety times that of Earth. Its fate was the same as all of the other Venera landers—after a brief span of activity, lasting about an hour, it ultimately melted and was crushed by the heat and pressure. Venus was a forbidding host.

American Missions to Venus

After a few false starts, the United States was ready to begin examining Venus as well. In August 1962, the United States launched *Mariner 2*. *Mariner 2* confirmed that Venus had an atmosphere composed mostly of carbon dioxide, that it was hotter than anyone had previously imagined, and that it had no magnetic field— a planet's magnetic field protects it from harmful solar radiation and is generated by the rotation of the planet and the movement of its liquid metal core.

The next U.S. probe was *Mariner 10*, which was launched on November 3, 1973. It flew by Venus on its way to Mercury. It took a

The *Mariner 10* spacecraft, shown here, was launched on November 3, 1973, from Cape Canaveral, Florida. On its way to Mercury, it passed Venus and studied the planet's atmosphere and temperature. Data from the mission revealed that there was little difference in temperature between the day side of Venus and the night side.

number of photographs of Venus's upper atmosphere, discovering that there was almost no difference in temperature between the day side of Venus and the night side.

In December 1978, the *Pioneer-Venus* craft reached Venus. *Pioneer-Venus* was made of one main probe and three smaller ones, which were all mounted on a central "bus." The bus released the probes over the atmosphere, allowing the scientists on Earth to get information from several locations on Venus simultaneously. These probes studied the composition of the atmosphere, collected information on the planet's gravity, and made the first accurate map of the surface of the planet.

Magellan

The most important satellite sent to Venus was *Magellan*. Although the *Pioneer-Venus* had made a map of Venus, and *Venera 15* and *Venera 16* had also mapped sections of Venus in 1984, *Magellan* was the first probe to provide a high-resolution image of the surface. Engaged in an elliptic orbit around Venus, *Magellan* began radar-mapping its surface in 1990. Since then we've discovered a wealth of information about the planet, from what its surface looks like to why it is so inhospitable to life. Thanks to *Magellan*, Venus is no longer a complete mystery.

Two

The Features of Venus

Venus is the second planet from the Sun, positioned between Mercury (the first) and Earth (the third). It is the second largest of the terrestrial planets and has no moons. Through an average-sized telescope, Venus appears as a brilliant, featureless sphere, hanging low in the sky. Blank, mysterious, and maddeningly close, our sister planet has been reluctant to reveal her secrets. In the past few decades, however, the satellites and landers sent to Venus have cleared up some of our misunderstandings and provided us with a lot of basic information that we were unable to collect before.

Two of a Kind

Venus has a diameter of about 7,520 miles (12,102 km), making it about 95 percent the size of Earth. Venus has a mass of about 4,870,000,000,000,000,000,000,000 kilograms. The shortened form of this number, written in a system called scientific notation, is 4.87×10^{24} kg. The exponent 24 indicates how many decimal places the number has. The mass of Venus is roughly 80 percent of Earth's.

The densities of Earth and Venus are also very similar. Venus has a density of 5.24 grams per cubic centimeter, whereas Earth has a density of 5.52 grams per cubic centimeter. Venus's gravity is about 90 percent of Earth's. So if you weighed 150 pounds (68 kg) on Earth, you'd weigh only about 135 pounds (61 kg) on Venus.

Most scientists agree that all of these similarities must mean that Venus's composition is nearly identical to Earth's. These similarities suggest that Venus probably has a core of iron and nickel about 1,865 miles (3,001 km) in diameter surrounded by a mantle of very dense rock. The lower mantle, closer to the center of the planet, is under a lot more pressure and is therefore rigid. The rock of the mantle is probably composed of silicate rocks, which are very rich in iron. A thin crust surrounds the mantle. Scientists think that Venus is less dense than Earth because of a concentration of sulfur, which has a fairly low density, at its core.

Venus in Orbit

If you observed Venus every night through a telescope, it would appear to move erratically through the sky. It appears this way because it is moving much more quickly than Earth, whipping around the Sun at 22 miles per second (35 km/sec), or 78,295 miles per hour (126,004 km/h).

A Giant Magnet

Planets are like gigantic magnets. They have a north pole and a south pole. Invisible lines of magnetic force come out of the north pole, loop through space, and enter the south pole. Magnetic fields are generated by a combination of the planet's rotation and fluid motion of the molten outer core of a planet. Venus's slow rotation means that the fluids of the outer core don't move very fast. As a result, the planet cannot generate a strong magnetic field.

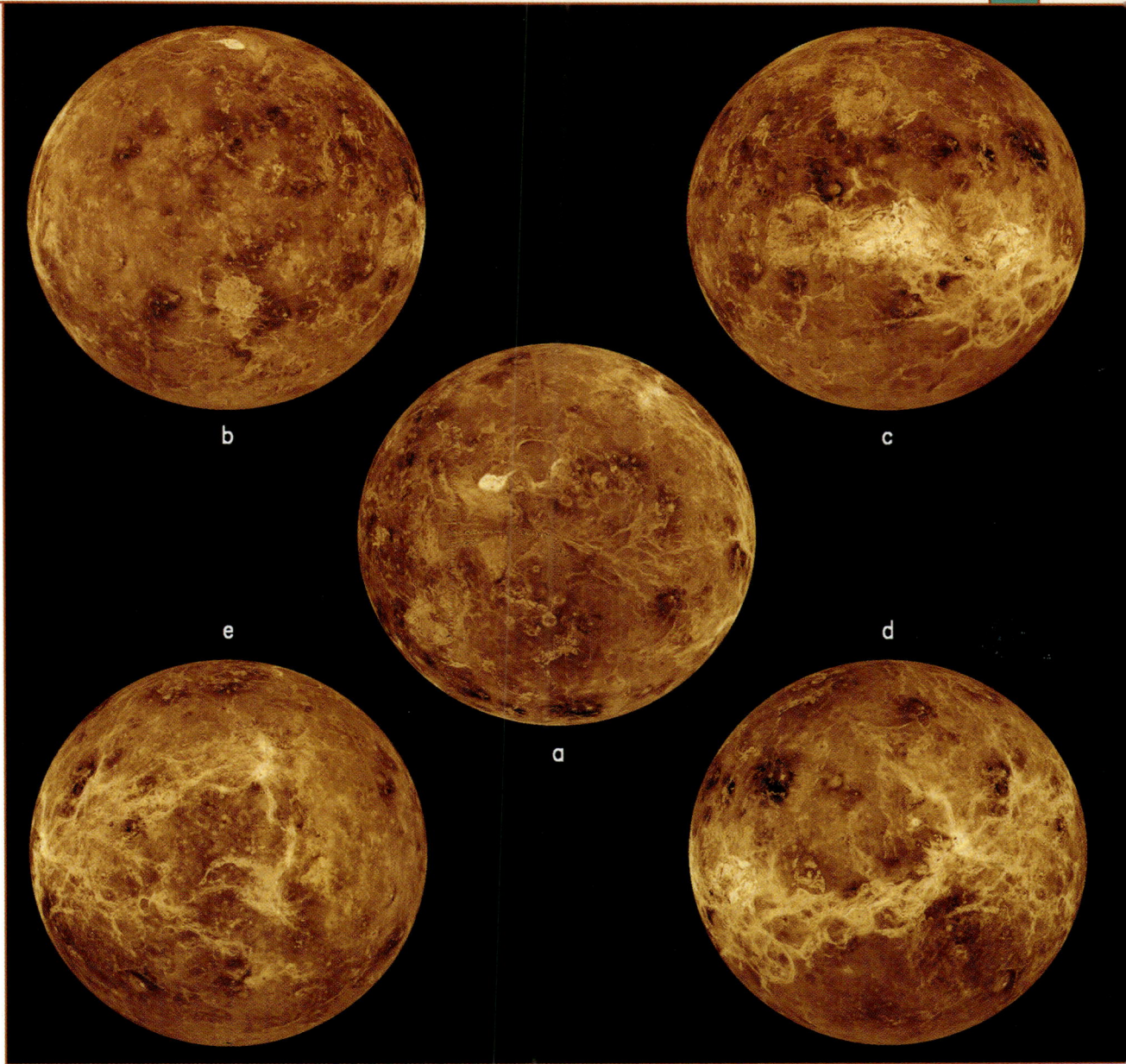

These radar images of Venus were made by the *Magellan* spacecraft between September 1990 and October 1994. Image a shows Venus's north pole. Images b, c, d, and e show different angles centered around Venus's equator. Image b is at 0° longitude. Image c is at 90° east longitude. Image d is at 180°. And image e is at 270° east longitude.

Planets that are closer to the Sun orbit more quickly than planets farther away. And just as Earth moves more quickly than any of the outer planets, Venus moves more quickly than Earth does. The reason for this is that the gravitational pull is stronger closer to the Sun.

Venus is only 67 million miles (108 million km) from the Sun, whereas Earth is 93 million miles (150 million km) away. If you can imagine the planets on their orbit around the Sun, Venus would be racing Earth around on the inside, just like one race car passing another.

As it is passing Earth, Venus is at its closest point to us, with only 26 million miles (42 million km) separating the two planets. When Venus is at its farthest, it is about 160 million miles (257 million km) away.

Spinning in Circles

Moving at the speed it does, Venus's year is only 224 Earth days long, compared to Earth's 365-day year. However, Venus rotates, or spins on its axis, very slowly, completing a rotation once every 243 days. This means that Venus's day is longer than its year.

Venus also has a retrograde rotation, which means that it spins in a clockwise direction as viewed from its north pole. Because of this, if you were standing on the surface of Venus (and were able to

Venus's Thin Waistline

Planets aren't perfect spheres, and they bulge a little at the sides from spinning on their axes, similar to the way a woman's skirt widens as she spins on a dance floor. Earth, for instance, is about 27 miles (43 km) wider at the equator than at the poles. Because Venus rotates so slowly, it has little bulge and is almost perfectly spherical.

see through the clouds), the Sun would rise in the west and set in the east. All planets orbit the Sun in a counterclockwise direction, and most (except for Uranus, Pluto, and Venus) also rotate the same way. No one is sure how Venus ended up with its odd rotation, although some scientists believe that a large asteroid may be the reason. They speculate that the asteroid collided with Venus and actually reversed its rotation.

A Different World

Although Venus and Earth share some compelling similarities, their differences couldn't be more pronounced. Venus and Earth took different paths when they began developing into the planets we know today. No one thought Venus would look exactly like Earth—no other planet does—but no one was prepared for what was found when *Magellan* began mapping the surface. Rather than a lush, life-supporting planet, we found a barren, fiery wasteland.

Three

An Unforgiving Landscape

If you were to stand on Venus, the ground under your feet would consist mainly of cracked red rocks. Everything, in fact, would have a red tint to it because the atmosphere filters out all incoming blue light. Depending on where you were standing, you might see a number of volcanoes oozing lava. There is never a break in the clouds overhead, and since every day on Venus is heavily overcast, the available light is about the same as on a very cloudy day on Earth. No matter where you went on the planet, you would never be able to see the Sun, sky, or stars.

Venus has an average surface temperature of about 900°F (485°C). If you were subjected to Venusian temperatures, the water in your cells would immediately boil and evaporate away. Since human beings are composed of about 80 percent water, whatever was left of you would be burnt to a cinder.

Even if a spacesuit were developed to counteract the heat, there would still be the immense atmospheric pressure to deal with. The weight of the Venusian atmosphere is roughly 1,300 pounds per square inch, or about ninety times that of Earth's atmospheric pressure of 14.7 pounds per square inch. Standing on Venus would be like diving to about 3,000 feet (914 meters) below the surface of the ocean, where the water pressure is equal to the atmospheric pressure of Venus. The pressure would immediately crush an astronaut and would probably crush his or her spacecraft shortly thereafter. It's no coincidence that the Soviet landers were modeled after deep-sea submarines, which are designed to withstand great amounts of pressure.

On April 28, 1989, the U.S. space shuttle *Atlantis* was launched into space, carrying *Magellan* with it. After its release, it took *Magellan* fifteen months to reach Venus. Arriving on August 10, 1990, it was captured by the planet's gravity and fell into an elliptical orbit around it. After a couple of minor technical difficulties, *Magellan* began the mapping process. By the time it burned up in Venus's atmosphere in October 1994, *Magellan* had mapped nearly the entire surface of the planet.

The *Magellan* spacecraft was launched from the cargo bay of the space shuttle *Atlantis* on May 4, 1989. It was the first spacecraft to be launched from the shuttle. It fell into an elliptical orbit around the planet. In the first eight months it collected images of nearly 85 percent of the planet's surface.

Venusian Volcanoes

One of the most striking pieces of information that *Magellan* sent back to us is that Venus has more volcanoes than anyone had ever imagined—more than Earth. In fact, 90 percent of Venus's surface is covered with volcanic landforms. Some of these volcanoes are hundreds of miles across and up to 5 miles (8 km) high. Smaller volcanoes tend to cluster into volcano fields. So far about 650 volcano fields have been identified, comprising more than 50,000 volcanoes.

The Sapas Mons volcano is located in Atla Regio, one of the many regions of Venus. It is approximately 2.8 miles (4.5 km) high and 249 miles (400 km) wide. The two dark areas near the center of the volcano are mesas. This image was altered by the *Magellan* radar, making the volcano look ten times taller than it really is.

The lava from these volcanoes flows in great "rivers," which eventually feed into the basalt "ocean" that comprises Venus's volcanic lowlands. These rivers are channels that are usually 1 mile (1.6 km) wide, and some of them are thousands of miles long. The longest of these rivers, called Baltis Vallis, is 4,200 miles (6,759 km) long, and some scientists think that it might be even longer.

Alien Landforms

Venus's volcanic activity has created a strange landscape unlike anything else in the solar system.

One landform that has no earthly equivalent is the corona. Coronae are formed by gigantic bubbles of magma. The magma slowly oozes up until it is underneath the planet's crust. The magma then swells until it pushes the crust up from underneath, forming a large swollen area on the surface. Eventually the magma inside cools and slowly sinks, leaving a depression.

Coronae can be circular mounds or depressions and are always surrounded by rings of fractures. Most coronae are between 100 and 200 miles (160 and 322 km) across, although some are even larger. The largest corona on the planet is called the Artemis Corona, which is more than 1,500 miles (2,414 km) across.

Venus hosts other strange volcanic landforms, which scientists are still studying. They are named after Earth's organisms, which they resemble. For example, anemones, or volcanoes with lava flows extending outward like feelers, are named after the flower-like sea creatures. Arachnoids are surrounded by jagged surface fractures that radiate outward. Ticks are volcanoes surrounded by ridges.

Another type of landform common to Venus is the pancake dome. Pancake domes are medium-sized volcanoes with steep sides and level tops, resembling single pancakes. Typically between 5 and 40 miles (8 and 64 km) across, more than 150 pancake domes have been identified on Venus's surface to date.

The Highlands

Highlands are the "continents" of Venus. They make up about 10 percent of Venus's surface area and are divided into three major regions. From east to west these regions are called Aphrodite Terra, Ishtar Terra, and Beta Regio.

Aphrodite Terra

Aphrodite Terra stretches along the equator of Venus and is roughly the size of Africa. It is so large that it encircles half the planet and hosts a variety of landforms.

Eastern Aphrodite is home to Atla Regio, a volcanic peak 1.8 miles (3 km) high. Atla Regio supports numerous volcanoes, the largest of which is Ozza Mons, which is 186 miles (300 km) across and 3.5 miles (5.6 km) high.

Moving westward over Aphrodite Terra, the land is compressed into troughs and ridges. The western side of Aphrodite Terra is comprised of the Ovda and Thetis regions, stretching for about 3,720 miles (5,987 km) and rising up to 2.5 miles (4 km) high. These two highlands are cut through by a number of faults and fractures.

Ishtar Terra

Thirty-eight hundred miles (6,116 km) wide and roughly the size of Australia, Ishtar Terra lies far north, near the pole. On its eastern side, Ishtar Terra contains Maxwell Montes, the highest point on all of Venus. A steeply elevated region, Maxwell Montes rises 7.5 miles (12 km) into the air and is dimpled by a large impact crater on it named Cleopatra, which is 65 miles (105 km) in diameter.

To the west of Maxwell Montes is the Lakshmi Planum, a plateau rising 2 miles (3.2 km) above the ground and spreading over an area of about 700,000 square miles (1,126,521 sq km).

Beta Regio

Beta Regio lies midway between the equator and the northern pole of Venus and is the site of the first Soviet spacecraft landing. It stretches 1,500 miles (2,414 km) from one end to the other. The

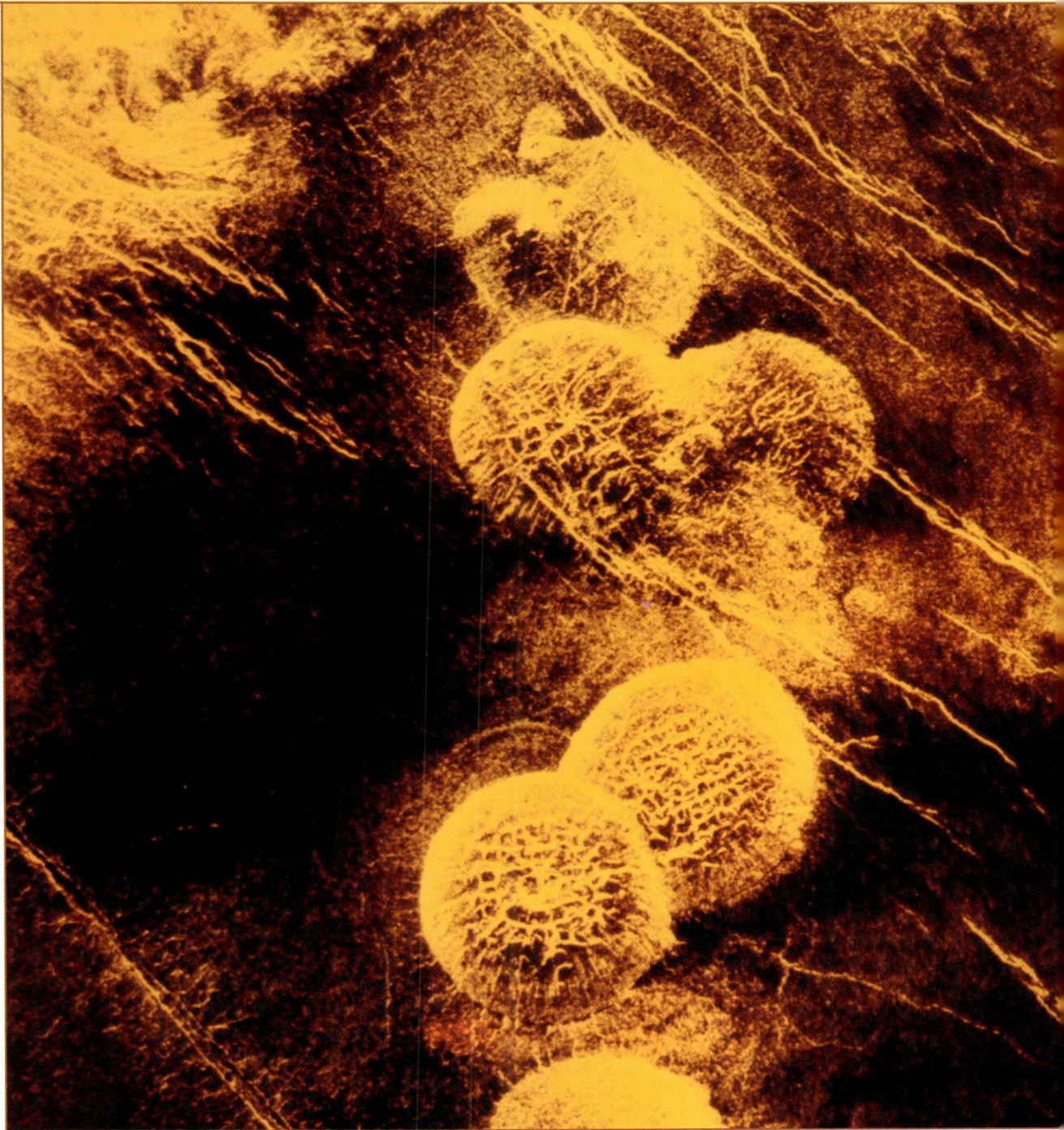

Lava from volcanic eruptions may have formed these dome-shaped hills in the Alpha Regio area of Venus. They are approximately 16 miles (26 km) across. It is believed by some scientists that the cooling of the lava may have formed these circular patterns. Another theory is that the domes were formed by lava from below the surface of Venus. This image was taken by the *Magellan* spacecraft in 1990.

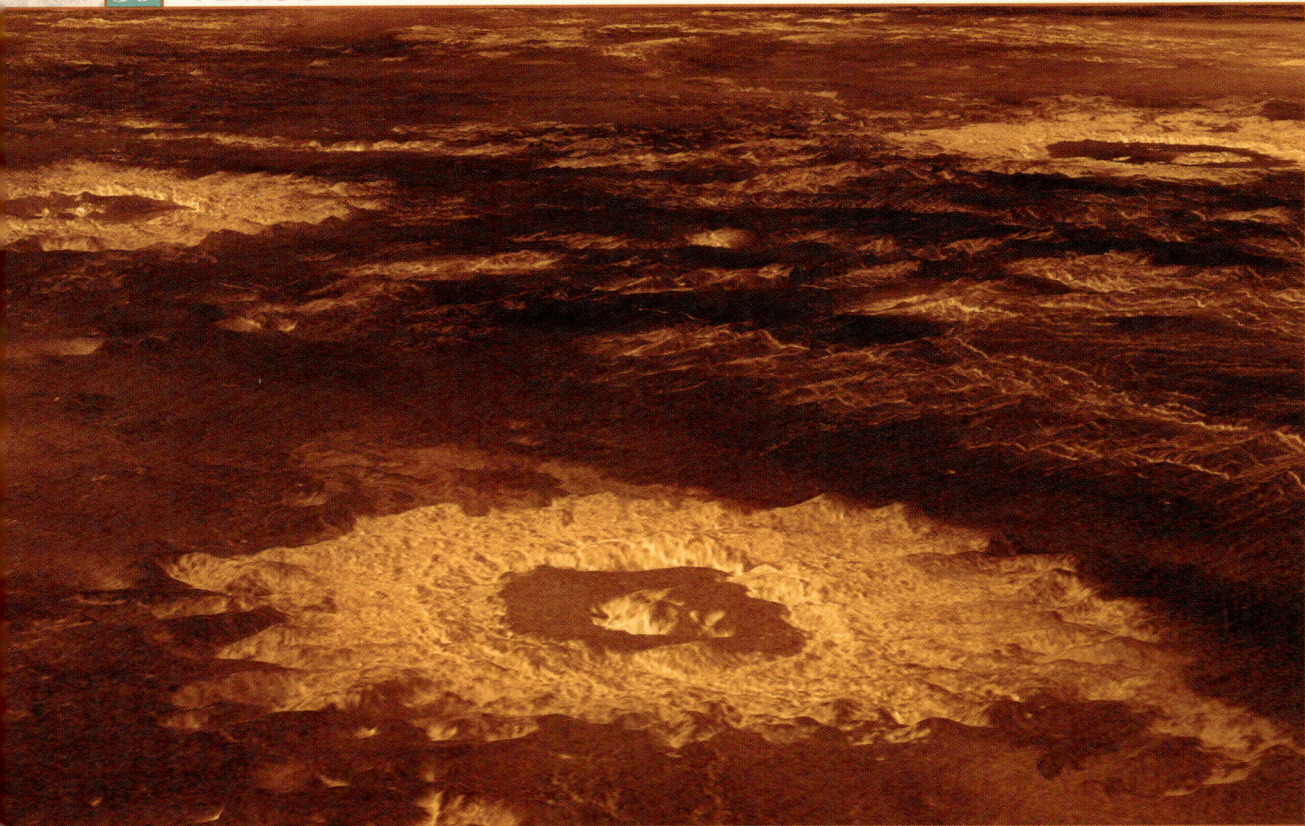

Howe Crater is located in a region of Venus called Lavinia Planitia, which was photographed along with the others by the *Magellan* spacecraft on November 7, 1991. Howe is 23 miles (37 km) wide. To the top left is Danilova Crater, which is 30 miles (48 km) wide. At the top right is Aglaonice Crater. It is 39 miles (63 km) wide. These craters were formed from objects impacting the surface of Venus.

region's most notable feature is a colossal volcano called Theia Mons, which is 3 miles (4.8 km) high and has a diameter of 215 miles (346 km).

A Young Face

Venus's strange, flowing landscape contains very few impact craters compared to Mercury, Mars, and the Moon. This is because asteroids and other space debris tend to burn up in the harrowing descent through the planet's atmosphere. An asteroid has to have an exceptionally large mass to get through. One strange thing scientists noticed when reviewing the data from *Magellan* is that all of the craters on the surface of Venus have sharp, clearly defined edges and all appear to be about the same age. A planet with craters will have some craters that are older and more eroded and some craters that are newer and virtually untouched. The craters on Venus, however, are all new. There are no old craters. The reason that there is very little erosion is because Venus has no vegetation, no water, and no precipitation reaching the surface.

There are about 900 craters on Venus, and scientists estimate that the surface is around half a billion years old. If this is true, where did the old surface go? The most commonly accepted explanation is that Venus used to undergo much more intense volcanic activity than it does now, and about a half a billion years ago, it completely flooded itself with lava. In other words, it effectively resurfaced itself. The face of Venus we see today is, on a geologic time scale, a relatively new one. We don't know what Venus looked like before this resurfacing, and we don't know what it will look like if another resurfacing takes place.

Four

Venus's Inhospitable Weather

Completely obscuring the sky, the atmosphere of Venus is remarkably poisonous and active. Although there is no inclement weather and little wind on the surface of the planet, there is a great deal of activity hidden among the clouds. At one time, scientists thought that there were constant lightning storms on Venus, but most scientists now think that this is unlikely. Even though Venus's atmosphere is poisonous to life, some scientists are hopeful that microbes might be discovered in the cooler upper atmosphere. However, the idea hasn't convinced many in the wider scientific community.

Besides being responsible for the great heat on Venus's surface, the atmosphere is also the greatest impediment to our continued observation of the planet. Space probes have to survive harsh winds and rain to land. If they ever make it to the ground, probes must contend with intense heat and overwhelming atmospheric pressure. Needless to say, no space agency has plans to land astronauts on Venus's surface any time soon.

Deadly Skies

Venus's atmosphere is composed of about 96.5 percent carbon dioxide and 3.5 percent nitrogen. The atmosphere also includes trace amounts of argon, carbon monoxide, helium, sulfur dioxide, and water.

Launched on November 3, 1973, *Mariner 10* took this image of Venus's atmosphere on February 5, 1974 on a flyby mission. Venus's thick atmosphere, shown here, traps heat and obscures the view of its surface. The planet's color was enhanced to make it appear as it would to the human eye.

Viewed through a powerful telescope, Venus's cloud cover is a featureless gray. When viewed with ultraviolet light, however, dark streaks can be seen winding their way through the clouds. Scientists think that these streaks are caused by other materials in the clouds that absorb ultraviolet light. Although the clouds are mainly composed of sulfuric acid (the same chemical found inside car batteries), they may also contain solid sulfur, sulfur dioxide, and chlorine.

Although Venus revolves very slowly, the upper cloud deck circles the planet every four days, spurred on by 225-mile-per-hour (362 km/h) winds. The wind on Venus is like this only in the upper reaches of the atmosphere—the breeze that blows on the surface is negligible.

The atmosphere traps and spreads the deadly heat of Venus, making both the day and night side of the planet incredibly hot. Things cool off the higher up you go, however. For example, the temperature is usually about 865°F (480°C) at 43 miles (69 km) above the surface. At 62 miles (100 km) above the surface, the temperature tops out at only about 77°F (25°C).

Acid Rain

Venus's atmosphere contains sulfur dioxide, which reacts to ultraviolet light from the Sun by breaking apart. After breaking up, the sulfur particles recombine with other chemicals in the atmosphere, eventually condensing and falling as acid. This acid rain is a major obstacle in sending spacecraft to Venus.

Human-produced carbon dioxide on Earth causes what is known as the greenhouse effect. The greenhouse effect is when heat becomes trapped in the atmosphere due to carbon dioxide. Many scientists fear that by continuing to pollute and add to the greenhouse effect, humans are virtually reproducing the atmosphere that Venus now has, where temperatures can reach 900°F (485°C).

The Greenhouse Effect

Venus's suffocating heat comes courtesy of an atmospheric process called the greenhouse effect. Every planet with an atmosphere, including Earth, has a greenhouse effect to some degree. With the greenhouse effect, different kinds of gases in the atmosphere absorb different types of radiation from the Sun. Most of the Sun's radiation passes through Venus's atmosphere without a problem. This radiation makes it to the planet's surface and is absorbed by the ground, heating the ground up. The ground then lets off its own radiation. Some of this radiation from the ground gets captured in the atmosphere, heating up the whole planet. On Earth, this process isn't very noticeable, but on Venus, it is extreme.

When coal, oil, and gasoline are burned on Earth, carbon dioxide is added to the atmosphere, accelerating the greenhouse effect and increasing global warming. The amount of carbon dioxide in Earth's atmosphere has increased by about 30 percent since the beginning of the 1800s. Many scientists are worried that if this is allowed to continue, Earth could someday become as inhospitable to life as Venus.

Five

Into the Future

Since *Magellan*, there haven't been any missions to Venus. The *Magellan* mission itself did not receive a lot of funding— the satellite was partially constructed of parts from other satellites to save money. Although NASA has no future missions to Venus scheduled, both Japan and the European Space Agency (ESA) are planning to send satellites there soon.

Japan is planning to send its probe to Venus some time in 2007. It will focus on analyzing the atmosphere, the mechanics of which are still not well understood by scientists. The ESA is planning to launch a satellite called the *Venus Express* in November 2005. The *Venus Express* is also going to examine Venus's atmosphere in an attempt to figure out why Earth and Venus, two planets that could hardly be more similar in size and composition, developed such radically different atmospheres.

That both of these missions have to do with Venus's atmosphere is no coincidence—changes in Earth's own atmosphere are becoming more noticeable due to carbon dioxide emissions and the greenhouse effect. As the controversy over pollution, which increases the greenhouse effect and causes global warming, rages on, planetary scientists will be looking toward Venus in an effort to better understand the greenhouse effect and its consequences.

As for Venus itself, it will go the way of all planets: eventually its interior will cool and it will slowly grow less and less active,

Venus Express is a spacecraft designed by the European Space Agency (ESA). It will be launched in November 2005. The mission will last 153 days, and the spacecraft will study Venus's atmosphere to figure out why this planet developed such a different atmosphere than Earth.

a process that will take hundreds of millions of years. While this is happening, the Sun will be growing more and more unstable.

In about 1 billion years, scientists think that the Sun might become more than 10 percent brighter than it is now. In about 4 billion years, it could become more than 40 percent brighter than it is now. In 5 billion years, the Sun will expand to about 100 times larger and 2,000 times brighter than it is now. Venus's atmosphere will evaporate, its surface will be scorched, and it will be consumed by the expanding Sun. In about 7 billion years, the nuclear reaction taking place within the Sun will cease. By that time, Venus will have become blended with the materials that make up the Sun, its atoms mingling with those of the other terrestrial planets, including Earth's.

Future Observation of Venus

Though the greenhouse effect can be harmful to Earth, it's also necessary for the existence of humankind. Earth is actually far enough from the Sun that, if things weren't being kept warm by the greenhouse effect, we would be trapped in a perpetual ice age. We've struck a near-perfect balance between too much carbon dioxide in the air, which would make Earth more like Venus, and too little, which would make Earth more like Mars, a cold planet.

Because burning fossil fuels puts more carbon dioxide into the atmosphere, the effects of global warming are increasing on Earth. Scientists estimate that the average temperature of Earth could rise from anywhere between 3°F to 10°F in the next hundred years. Although that may not sound like much, it could cause catastrophic changes in Earth's climate, making the weather erratic and unpredictable, as well as melting the polar ice caps and causing the ocean levels to rise.

Global warming is not only a threat to humankind but also to the billions of plant and animal species on Earth. Venus is the best example we have of a place where global warming is extreme, and Earth is the best (and only) example we have of a planet sustaining the delicate equilibrium necessary to support life.

Venus has a lot to teach us about Earth, and scientists are still trying to discover if, through human irresponsibility, Earth will someday look like Venus. The more we learn about our sister planet, the more we'll learn about ourselves.

1961: Soviet Union sends *Venera 1* to Venus on February 12, which loses contact with Earth on the way and is presumably in orbit around the Sun.

1962: The United States launches *Mariner 2* to Venus in August. *Mariner 2* confirms that Venus has an atmosphere composed mostly of carbon dioxide, that it is hotter than anyone had previously imagined, and that it has almost no magnetic field.

1965: Soviet Union launches *Venera 3* on November 12 with the mission objective of landing on Venus's surface. It loses contact with Earth just as it makes it through Venus's atmosphere. It crash-lands on the surface on March 1, 1966, and is destroyed.

1969: Soviet Union launches *Venera 5* and *Venera 6* in January. These spacecraft eventually enter Venus's atmosphere.

1970: Soviet Union launches *Venera 7* in August. *Venera 7* lands on the surface and sends back information for twenty-three minutes.

1973: United States' *Mariner 10* flies by Venus on its way to Mercury and takes a number of photographs of Venus's upper atmosphere.

1975: Soviet Union launches *Venera 9* and *Venera 10* in August. These spacecraft land on Venus and send back one photograph each.

1978: United States' *Pioneer-Venus* reaches Venus in December. It makes the first accurate map of the surface of the planet.

1981: Soviet Union's *Venera 14* touches down on Venus on November 4.

2005: The European Space Agency (ESA) plans to launch a satellite called the *Venus Express* in November.

2007: Japan plans to send its probe to Venus.

Glossary

codexes Manuscripts or books.

diameter The length of a straight line through the center of an object.

greenhouse effect The process by which a planet's temperature increases due to atmospheric absorption of solar radiation and the blocking of thermal radiation emitted from the planet's surface.

heliocentric Centered around the Sun.

lava Molten rock extruded from the interior of a planet onto its surface.

magma Molten rock beneath the surface of a planet.

mons A term for a mountain.

regio Another term for a region.

retrograde Having a direction opposite to the motion of similar bodies.

terra Another term for a large landmass.

For More Information

Adler Planetarium & Astronomy Museum
1300 S. Lake Shore Drive
Chicago, IL 60605-2403
(312) 922-STAR (7827)
e-mail: AskAdler@adlernet.org
Web site: http://www.adlerplanetarium.org

The Planetary Society
65 North Catalina Avenue
Pasadena, CA 91106-2301
(626) 793-5100
e-mail: tps@planetary.org
Web site: http://www.planetary.org

Smithsonian National Air and Space Museum
Seventh and Independence Avenue SW
Washington, DC 20560
(202) 357-2700
e-mail: info@info.si.edu
Web site: http://www.nasm.si.edu

Web Sites

Due to the changing nature of Internet links, the Rosen Publishing Group, Inc., has developed an online list of Web sites related to the subject of this book. This site is updated regularly. Please use this link to access the list:

http://www.rosenlinks.com/lnp/venu

For Further Reading

Brimner, Larry Dane. *Venus* (True Books: Space). New York: Children's Press: 1998.

Gallan, Roy A. *The Planets: Exploring the Solar System*. New York: Four Winds Press, 1982.

Roop, Peter, and Connie Roop. *The Solar System: Opposing Viewpoints*. San Diego: Greenhaven Press, Inc. 1988.

Simon, Seymour. *Venus*. New York: William Morrow, 1992.

Vogt, Gregory. *Magellan and the Mapping of Venus*. Brookfield, CT: The Millbrook Press, 1992.

Bibliography

Cattermole, Peter, and Patrick Moore. *Atlas of Venus*. Cambridge, UK: Cambridge University Press, 1997.

Frankel, Charles. *Volcanoes of the Solar System*. Cambridge, UK: Cambridge University Press, 1996.

Friedel, David, Joy Parker, and Linda Schele. *Maya Cosmos*. New York: Quill, 1993.

Grinspoon, David Harry. *Venus Revealed: A New Look Below the Clouds of Our Mysterious Twin Planet*. Boston: Addison-Wesley Publishing Company, Inc., 1997.

"Greenhouse Effects . . . Also on Other Planets." European Space Agency. February 14, 2003. Retrieved September, 2002. (http://www.sci.esa.int/science-e-www/object/index.cfm?fobjectid=32528).

"Japan Plans 2007 Mission to Venus." Space.com. May 2, 2001. Retrieved September 5, 2003. (http://www.space.com/missionlaunches/missions/japan_venus_plans_010502.html)

Marov, Mikhail Ya., and David H. Grinspoon. *The Planet Venus*. New Haven, CT: Yale University Press, 1998.

Radford, Tim. "Mission to Venus Could Explain Greenhouse Effect." Guardian.co.uk. August 6, 2001. Retrieved September, 2001. (http://www.guardian.co.uk/uk_news/story/0,3604,532319,00.html).

Taylor, F. W. *The Cambridge Photographic Guide to the Planets*. Cambridge, UK: Cambridge University Press, 2001.

Tedlock, Dennis. *Popol Vuh*. New York: Simon & Schuster, Inc., 1985.

"Venus." Britannica.com. Retrieved September 5, 2003. (http://www.search.eb.com/eb/article?eu=118796).

"Venus Mission Is On." News.bbc.com. November 8, 2003. Retrieved September, 2002. (http://www.news.bbc.co.uk/1/hi/sci/tech/2421665.stm)

Watters, Thomas R. *Smithsonian Guides: Planets*. New York: Macmillan, 1995.

Index

About the Author

R. K. Renfield is a freelance writer who lives in New York State.

Credits

Designer: Thomas Forget; Editor: Nicholas Croce